CRIME SCIENCE

HOMICIDE

Angela Royston

Gareth Stevens
Publishing

Please visit our website, www.garethstevens.com. For a free color catalog of all our high-quality books, call toll free 1-800-542-2595 or fax 1-877-542-2596.

Library of Congress Cataloging-in-Publication Data

Royston, Angela.
Homicide / by Angela Royston.
  p. cm. -- (Crime science)
Includes index.
ISBN 978-1-4339-9493-7 (pbk.)
ISBN 978-1-4339-9494-4 (6-pack)
ISBN 978-1-4339-9492-0 (library binding)
1. Murder — Investigation — Juvenile literature. 2. Homicide investigation—Juvenile literature. I. Royston, Angela, 1945- II. Title.
HV6515.R69 2014
364.152—dc23

First Edition

Published in 2014 by
Gareth Stevens Publishing
111 East 14th Street, Suite 349
New York, NY 10003

© 2014 Gareth Stevens Publishing

Produced by Calcium, www.calciumcreative.co.uk
Designed by Keith Williams and Paul Myerscough
Edited by Sarah Eason and Jennifer Sanderson

Photo credits: Cover: Shutterstock: Joe Belanger tl, Corepics VOF br. Inside: Dreamstime: Allein 9b, Aniram 8, Eddiesimages 9t; Shutterstock: Benjamin Albiach Galan 20, Anton Prado Photo 4, Anyaivanova 21, Arena Creative 5b, Joe Belanger 11, Joerg Beuge 32, Sascha Burkard 1, 28, Kevin L Chesson 10, 27, Corepics VOF 33, Ded Pixto 7, Jack Dagley Photography 6, Dragon Images 44, Faraways 15t, Kellie L. Folkerts 25, Zack Frank 31, Glyphstock 5t, IM Photo 12, Fisun Ivan 34, Kanusommer 37, Zoran Karapancev 39, Peter Kim 29, Kuzma 22t, Daryl Lang 17, Monkey Business Images 42, Netfalls Remy Musser 26, Newton Page 13, Noel Powell 40, Matee Nuserm 23, Richard A. McGuirk 24, Adam Radosavljevic 43, Ruigsantos 19, Henryk Sadura 38, Guy J. Sagi 30, Sheff 41, Kenneth Sponsler 14, Tarasov 22b, Leah-Anne Thompson 15b, 16l, 18, Tlorna 35b, Trubach 45, Mik Ulyannikov 36, Martin D. Vonka 35t.

Printed in the United States of America

CPSIA compliance information: Batch #CS13GS: For further information contact Gareth Stevens, New York, New York at 1-800-542-2595.

CONTENTS

WHAT IS HOMICIDE?

Homicide is the killing of one person by another person. When the killing is deliberate, the crime is murder. Manslaughter is accidental or unintentional homicide, perhaps committed in self-defense or in a fight that got out of hand. Homicide is one of the most serious offenses. In some countries, certain types of murder carry the death penalty.

Investigating a Killing

Two groups of people investigate homicide—the police and forensic scientists. The police interview witnesses, find out who the victim is, and try to identify and arrest the killer. The police need to prove that he or she is the killer, and this is where forensic scientists can be critical in solving a case.

Forensic Scientists

Scientists who specialize in crime are called forensic scientists. Their job is to find and examine evidence to help the police piece together what happened. They also help to identify criminals. If a suspect is arrested, the forensic scientists' evidence may confirm whether or not he or she is the killer.

As soon as a homicide is reported to the police, police cars rush to the crime scene.

CRACKED

Most victims know their killer, so police usually look for a murderer among people known to the victim. Around one-fifth of victims are women, of whom between around half and three-quarters are killed by their family or by their partner.

Number of Homicides

The United States has one of the highest rates of homicide in the developed world. Most murders take place in the country's big cities, but these have been falling. The total number has fallen from 23,400 in 1990 to just over half that number in 2011.

If a suspect is found at, or near, the crime scene, he or she is immediately arrested.

News of a murder is reported by newspapers and other media.

Shot To Death

On Saturday, the response... New Haven. Teams of dete... the neighborhood aro... Street looking for lea... day said they had... sible suspects. ... and ... ron of Ja...

...rked the first time ...that someone so shooting in ...aturday. ...ttrac- ...ti-

CHAPTER ONE

INVESTIGATING A HOMICIDE

A body has been found—the police are called to the scene of a possible murder. How do they find the killer? First they examine the body and check whether the killer is still at the scene. Then they interview witnesses and start to figure out what happened. They call in forensic scientists to collect evidence and analyze it in microscopic detail.

Examining the Body

The first person at the crime scene checks whether the victim is still breathing, and whether he or she has a pulse. If the investigator is sure the victim is dead, he or she will try to establish the cause of death. It the person has been shot, stabbed, or hit with a heavy object, investigators must look for the weapon.

A body is covered by a plastic sheet until it is examined by a forensic scientist.

Investigating the Crime Scene

Even if a police officer is sure about the cause of death, the body needs to be examined by a forensic scientist. The forensic scientist will then collect further evidence, such as samples of blood. Other forensic scientists photograph and record every piece of evidence collected.

The Crime Lab

The evidence collected at the crime scene is taken to the police laboratory, or lab. Here it is examined in more detail. Any weapons are checked for fingerprints, and samples of blood are compared under a microscope.

CRACKED

Police interview witnesses who may have seen the attack or something suspicious. Someone may know the victim, for example, or have seen the possible killer running away. Evidence from witnesses can be extremely valuable, but a crime can happen so quickly that witnesses can be mistaken.

Blood and other material collected at the crime scene are tested in the police laboratory.

THE CRIME SCENE

The crime scene is the place where the crime occurred. In a murder, this is often where the body is found. There may, however, be more than one crime scene, because the victim may have been attacked in one place and the body left or buried elsewhere. A murder investigation starts where the body is found.

Securing the Crime Scene

As soon as the police arrive, one of the officers secures the crime scene. This may be part of the street or another outdoor area. It could also be a room, or even an entire building. The crime scene contains evidence that must not be lost or disturbed, so the whole scene is immediately sealed off, and the public are kept out.

Examining the Scene

When the forensic scientists arrive, they examine and photograph everything that may be connected to the killing. The photographs show exactly where each piece of evidence was found. Everything at a crime scene can be important. Murderers often leave clues without realizing it. They may leave footprints, fingerprints, or tiny threads from their clothes.

Forensic scientists examine every square inch of a crime scene looking for evidence.

2

Every piece of evidence at a crime scene is numbered and photographed.

Preserving the Evidence

Every piece of evidence that is collected is placed in a separate, clean bag to make sure that it is not contaminated with blood or other evidence. For the same reason, crime scene investigators wear gloves and special clothes.

BACK IN THE LAB

After the body has been examined and photographed, it is placed in a body bag and taken to the autopsy room. There, forensic pathologists examine it to find out more about the cause of death. They also try to figure out the time of death.

Bodies recovered from a crime scene are examined in an autopsy room.

9

THE FORENSIC TEAM

Forensic scientists collect and analyze evidence. Many different forensic specialists may be involved in solving a crime. There are two main groups—crime scene investigators who focus on different aspects of the crime scene and others who work mainly in the crime lab.

Crime Scene Investigators

Crime scene investigators are responsible for identifying and collecting evidence at the crime scene. They include fingerprint specialists, photographers, and firearms specialists.

Crime Laboratories

The evidence collected at the crime scene is analyzed in the crime lab. Scientists in different departments within the lab concentrate on particular aspects, such as the body, blood, DNA, bullets, and weapons. They use special equipment and advanced scientific techniques to carry out their jobs.

A special light is used to detect fingerprints on any objects found at the crime scene.

Staged Crime Scenes

Crime scene investigators have to be on the lookout for staged crime scenes. These are crime scenes that have been altered to make it look as if something other than the crime happened. If a gun is put into the hand of a dead victim, a murder might be disguised as a suicide.

REAL-LIFE CASE

In the 1920s, Chicago was racked by battles between rival criminal gangs. One of the worst incidents occurred on Valentine's Day in 1929. Seven members of Bugs Moran's gang were gunned down by two men in police uniform. The bullet casings were the same type as those used by the Chicago Police Department. Did the police shoot the gang? Forensic firearms expert Calvin Goddard tested every gun owned by the police department and was able to declare that none of them had been used in the massacre. Then the search for the real gunmen began!

DATABASES

A database is a collection of information that is stored on a computer. It is organized so that any particular item can be easily found. Police departments keep information about convicted criminals and about crimes. When a crime is committed they can search databases for similarities to past crimes.

Identifying Criminals

For decades, the police have kept photographs of convicted criminals. They have also kept copies of their fingerprints. These are stored on databases and can be easily accessed so that fingerprints found on a knife, for example, can be checked to see if they match fingerprints on the database. Today, the police record other identifying features, too.

Detectives have access to huge amounts of information stored on computer databases.

Identifying Marks

All vehicles carry a license plate. If the police know the license plate number of a vehicle seen near the killing, they can search a database to trace the number and the owner of the vehicle. Guns also have distinctive marks (see page 30), which can be recorded and stored on a computer.

Similar Crimes

Apart from identifying particular features about the killer, investigators study the way the crime was carried out. Murderers who have killed other victims often go about their crimes in a similar way. For example, they use the same type of weapon and attack a similar type of victim in the same way. Using computers, investigators search for similarities with other attacks.

CRACKED

Forensic scientists are now able to analyze and identify much more evidence than they previously could. For example, they can now identify people through samples of blood (see page 18). By reexamining evidence collected many years ago, they can then sometimes crack previously unsolved cases.

13

CHAPTER TWO
IDENTIFYING INDIVIDUALS

Everyone is unique. The 6 billion people in the world are all different in various ways that can be detected and recorded. Although identical twins look alike, they have unique differences, such as their fingerprint patterns. Police use these differences to identify people involved in a crime.

Changing Appearance

It is possible for criminals to change their appearance. Many witnesses have only a fleeting glimpse of a killer and tend to remember things, such as clothes, which are easy to change. A different hairstyle or hair color quickly alters someone's appearance. For a man, shaving off or growing a beard changes the look of his face.

Distinguishing Features

Forensic scientists look for the features that cannot be changed. In particular, they examine the crime scene for fingerprints, blood, and traces of DNA. It is only in the last 30 years that forensic scientists have been able to test for DNA. These are the chemicals inside each cell which, among other things, determine how we look.

At first glance, it is hard to tell identical twins apart, but forensic scientists can distinguish between them.

Still Identifiable

Once a person is dead, his or her body begins to decompose. Although decomposed and very badly damaged bodies are more difficult to identify, many of their distinguishing features may remain. For example, teeth can last for centuries, so police can check the dental records of a missing person to see if they match the victim's teeth.

Everyone is different from everyone else and from everyone who has ever lived.

A forensic scientist uses a special magnifying glass to examine a bloodstained shirt.

CRACKED

Everybody has the same number of teeth but everyone's teeth are slightly different in size and shape. Most people have one or two teeth that are not perfectly aligned. Other teeth may be chipped or missing. Dental records reveal all the details of a person's teeth and can be used to identify people.

FINGERPRINTS

The fine ridges on your fingertips help you to feel surfaces and to pick up small things. The ridges form a pattern of arches, loops, or whorls. Every finger has a different pattern, which stays the same throughout your life. When you touch a hard, smooth surface, you leave behind a copy of your own unique patterns—your fingerprints.

Detecting Fingerprints

At the crime scene, some fingerprints may be clearly visible, especially if they were made by someone with grease, dirt, or blood on their hands. Many others will not be visible. Forensic scientists use fine powder or special lights to reveal hidden prints. They examine likely surfaces, such as weapons, doors, and window frames. Once the prints are visible, they are photographed or lifted using a piece of transparent tape.

Around one-third of fingerprints are whorls, but the exact pattern of each print varies.

Fingerprints are slightly oily, so fine, black powder sticks to them.

Getting a Clear Print

Doors and similar surfaces are covered with many different people's fingerprints. A lot of the prints will be smudged or partly covered by other prints. A crime scene investigator will try to find one or two clear prints. Digital cameras and computer software make this easier than it used to be. Today, investigators can sharpen up prints before they try to match them with known prints.

President John F. Kennedy was assassinated by shots fired from the sixth floor of the Texas School Book Depository in Dallas, Texas.

REAL-LIFE CASE

As well as fingerprints, toe prints, ear prints, and palm prints are also unique. In 1963, President John F. Kennedy was shot as he drove in an open car through Dallas, Texas. The shots came from a particular building, the Texas School Book Depository. When police searched the building, they found a rifle with a palm print on it. The palm print was matched to that of Lee Harvey Oswald, who was arrested for the crime.

17

BLOODSTAINS

Blood is extremely useful to forensic scientists. They take samples from the victim and look for bloodstains on walls, on the ground, on clothes, and on the weapon. Killers often try to get rid of bloodstains by washing or dumping the items, so police search trash cans and other waste for abandoned clothes and weapons.

Is It Blood?

First scientists test their samples to see whether the stains are in fact blood. Certain chemicals change color or glow when mixed with blood. For example, luminol glows when it reacts with even a tiny amount of blood. It can also detect blood on surfaces that have been cleaned or painted over.

These stains on a T-shirt are tested to see if they are blood and then matched to other blood samples.

Identifying Blood

Once the presence of human blood is confirmed, the scientists try to identify whose blood it is. There are four main blood groups—O, A, B, and AB. The blood group of each sample can be useful in distinguishing the victim's blood from other sources of blood. A blood-group match does not necessarily identify a particular person: only DNA can do that.

Bleeding to Death

The amount of blood reveals information about the killing. Bleeding stops as soon as a person's heart stops beating. A person who dies instantly sheds very little blood. A lot of blood, however, suggests that the victim was wounded for some time before he or she died.

A sample of blood can give forensic scientists vital information about the crime.

CRACKED

The pattern of a bloodstain helps crime investigators to reconstruct the crime. If the blood is spattered into many tiny drops, they use string to trace each drop back to the point where they all meet. This tells them where the victim was when he or she was shot or hit.

DNA—THE ULTIMATE IDENTIFIER

Your body is made up of trillions of tiny cells. Different types of cells make up your skin, for example, or your heart, but every cell contains the same DNA. Every person's DNA is different. Being able to match DNA to a particular person has made identifying criminals much easier.

Detecting DNA

Wherever you go and whatever you touch, you leave behind a trace of DNA. Whole hairs and flakes of skin fall from your body. Body fluids, particularly blood, saliva (spit), and sweat, all contain DNA. Crime scene investigators look at everything for traces of DNA.

This model shows the structure of the DNA molecule.

BACK IN THE LAB

In the past, many samples of DNA were too small to analyze. However, scientists now copy small samples to give an enhanced sample with which to work. The enhanced sample is not as reliable as a genuinely large sample, however, because any mistakes present in the small sample are copied, too.

Taking Samples

Investigators have to be extremely careful when collecting samples. Just a few cells contain enough DNA to identify an individual, but only if the sample has been correctly stored and preserved. They have to make sure that the sample is not contaminated by their own DNA, or by other evidence from the crime scene or the lab.

Matching Samples

At the lab, forensic scientists analyze the DNA sample and turn it into a pattern of gray bands, which they print out. Scientists compare the patterns from two samples to see if they match. They may compare DNA collected at the crime scene with DNA in a database, or they may compare it with a fresh sample from a suspect.

Forensic scientists must take great care when testing samples.

CIRCUMSTANTIAL EVIDENCE

Circumstantial evidence, such as footprints or threads of cloth, shows a possible link between a suspect and the crime scene. For example, if a footprint matches a shoe found at a suspect's home, it indicates that the suspect could have made it. Circumstantial evidence is not proof, however, because other people may have the same type of shoe.

Tire treads leave very clear prints in freshly fallen snow.

Treads

Shoes and tires both have treads to grip the ground better. Different types of shoe and tire have particular patterns of tread. Tread marks can link a suspect to a crime scene. If the ground is wet and muddy, investigators may find footprints indoors or tire prints outdoors. In addition, scientists may be able to match grains of mud or grit stuck in the treads to mud or grit at the crime scene.

The treads on these sneakers will produce distinctive, but not unique, footprints.

The wool or fiber used to knit a scarf or sweater is made of small, thin strands twisted together.

Threads

Cloth is woven from threads of cotton, wool, or synthetic material. The threads consist of many tiny strands twisted together. When cloth is rubbed—during a struggle, for example—some of the strands may cling to the victim. Using a special microscope, scientists can compare fibers found at the crime scene with fibers from the suspect's clothes. If they match, the suspect could be the killer.

REAL-LIFE CASE

In 2004, Scott Peterson was convicted of murdering his wife, who had disappeared in 2002 in California. The evidence against him was powerful, but almost all of it was circumstantial. For example, two weeks before she disappeared, Peterson told a new girlfriend that he had "lost his wife," which suggested he was planning to murder her. He also sold his wife's car before her body was discovered.

CHAPTER THREE

IDENTIFYING THE WEAPON

Some murderers kill with their hands or feet, but most use a weapon. Weapons include guns and switchblades, which are designed to harm people, but everyday objects can also be turned into lethal weapons. Kitchen knives, baseball bats, and many kinds of heavy objects can become murder weapons.

Finding the Weapon

Sometimes the weapon is found at the crime scene, but not usually. Finding the weapon is a crucial step to finding the killer. Many killers try to get rid of the weapon to avoid being caught with it. They may drop it close to the crime scene as they run away, or they may throw it in a river or lake. They may even try to wipe it clean of fingerprints and throw it in a trash can.

Police divers search for missing weapons at the bottom of rivers, lakes, and ponds.

Empty shells and cartridges give vital clues to the type of gun used to fire them.

BACK IN THE LAB

Identifying Missing Weapons

Even if the weapon is missing, there may be clues at the crime scene. With many guns, a shell case drops to the ground when a bullet is fired. Since different types of gun use different cartridges, the shell case and the bullets can indicate the type of gun used.

A pathologist can learn a great deal about a weapon from the size and shape of the victim's wounds. A bullet may enter the body and become lodged, or it may leave the body through an exit hole. The shape of a knife wound can indicate the size and type of knife used.

Most Common Weapon

Guns are the most common murder weapons used in the United States, probably because they kill quickly and can be used from a distance. They account for around twice as many deaths as all the other weapons put together.

GUNS

There are two main types of guns—handguns and rifles. Handguns are small enough to conceal on the body and can be fired with one hand. They include revolvers and pistols, and account for around three-quarters of fatal shootings. Rifles are larger, with a long barrel, making them more accurate from a distance.

Law enforcers fire at targets to improve their gun skills. Using two hands gives greater accuracy with a handgun.

How a Gun Works

When a gunman pulls the trigger of a gun, a bullet is released. It spins at high speed toward the target. The bullet is loaded into the gun in a cartridge, which contains gunpowder. Pulling the trigger ignites the gunpowder so that it explodes and forces the bullet down the gun's barrel. The empty cartridge—the shell case—falls to the ground.

Smoking Gun?

When a gun is fired, most of the gases and particles from the explosion escape down the barrel. This has given rise to the idea of "a smoking gun." Although the gases disappear in an instant, they often leak out, spraying a powder called gunshot residue over the killer and the surroundings.

A gunshot-residue test is carried out on a suspect's left hand.

REAL-LIFE CASE

In 1967, John Branion, a doctor in Chicago, discovered his wife's dead body, which had been shot several times. A forensic scientist examined the shell cases and bullets and said that they came from a Walther PPK. Branion claimed that he did not own such a gun. When police searched his home, however, they found ammunition for a Walther PPK and references to a gun with a particular serial number. They traced the serial number and found it was from a Walther PPK that had been given to Branion as a present. Branion was convicted of the murder.

LEFT PALM

RECONSTRUCTING THE CRIME

Police do not only want to prove that a particular suspect is the killer, they also want to figure out exactly how the killing happened and how many people were involved. This is important in deciding whether to charge the suspect with murder or manslaughter.

Examining the Victim

Gunshot wounds on the victim's body can reveal a lot of information. For example, if gunshot residue is found around the bullet wound, it shows that the killer was fewer than 2 feet (0.6 m) from the victim when the gun was fired. By looking at the entry wound and the exit wound, if there is one, a firearms expert can calculate the angle at which the bullet entered the body.

Tracking the Bullet

A bullet may ricochet off a wall or furniture before or after hitting the victim. Crime scene investigators look for nicks in furniture and dents in walls to help them reconstruct the path of the bullet. They may use string to trace the path of the bullet back from the body to figure out where the gunman was standing.

When a bullet passes through glass, it leaves a hole surrounded by a circle of shattered glass.

An investigator helps to reconstruct the crime scene, showing exactly how the body and the empty shell cases were found.

The Full Picture

A killer may fire several shots from one position, or the gunman or the victim may move during the attack. There may have been more than one gunman, or the killer may have used more than one gun. The victim, too, may have fired a shot. It takes patient forensic work to reconstruct a crime.

CRACKED

Even if the crime scene investigators do not find any weapons, they collect all the bullets and shell casings that they find. These not only tell them how many guns were used, but they also help them to reconstruct the crime.

IDENTIFYING THE GUN

Forensic scientists can do more than identify the type of gun used—they can link a bullet to a particular gun. This is because the barrel of a gun leaves a distinct pattern on a bullet, called rifling marks.

Rifling Marks

Most guns are designed to make the bullet spin as it whistles through the air. Spinning keeps the bullet moving straight along its path.

The bullet is spun by a spiral of grooves cut into the inside of the barrel of the gun. The grooves scratch the bullet, leaving what is known as rifling marks on the bullet.

A spiral of grooves inside the barrel of a gun leaves a unique pattern on the bullet.

Comparing Bullets

Each machine in a gun factory makes a particular pattern of grooves, so each type of gun has a distinctive rifling pattern. In addition, the gun-making machine wears as it is used, changing the grooves slightly in each new gun. This means that the rifling marks produced are a little different each time, so a bullet can be uniquely identified with a particular gun.

Comparison Microscope

A comparison microscope allows two things, such as bullets or threads of cloth, to be compared side by side. It was first used in the United States in 1927 by a gun expert named Calvin Goddard to prove that a suspect was guilty (see Real-Life Case below).

The J. Edgar Hoover Building in Washington, DC, is the headquarters of the FBI. Goddard helped the FBI to set up the first national forensic laboratory in 1932.

REAL-LIFE CASE

Calvin Goddard was asked to help in a case that hinged on whether the gun of the accused man, Nicola Sacco, had been used to murder two payroll guards. In court, Goddard took Sacco's gun and fired it into cotton wool. He placed the bullet in the comparison microscope next to the bullet from the murder. The rifling marks on both were clearly the same, proving the prosecution's case.

KNIVES AND SHARP IMPLEMENTS

Forensic scientists cannot identify a particular knife or sharp implement, such as a screwdriver, as the murder weapon unless the victim's blood is found on it. Instead the investigators rely on the pathologist for information revealed by the wounds on the body to help them to reconstruct what happened.

Stab Wounds

The type of wound inflicted depends on how a weapon is used. Sharp blades, such as knives and swords, are often used to stab a victim. A stab wound is usually as wide as the blade and can go deep into the victim's body. A deep cut is likely to damage a vital organ, such as the heart, lungs, or liver, or to cut an artery. A killer or group of killers may stab several times before leaving the victim to bleed to death.

A sharp kitchen knife is useful for cutting up vegetables, but it can also be used as a lethal weapon.

An autopsy describes every wound found on the body. The depth of a wound shows how the weapon was wielded. The angle of a stab wound helps forensic scientists to figure out where the killer was in relation to the victim—for example, whether the attacker stood in front, behind, or above the victim.

A knife and cigarette stub are numbered and photographed before being taken from the crime scene to the lab.

Cuts and Chops

Knives are also used to cut the skin. The kind of cut can tell investigators something about the crime. If the victim tried to fight off the attacker, his or her hands and arms may have cuts. If the body shows a deep, wedge-shaped wound, it could mean that the killer used an ax or similar heavy chopping weapon.

BLUNT IMPLEMENTS

Killers do not always spill blood. Hitting a victim with a blunt implement, such as a baseball bat, or a heavy object can kill, too. Blows to the body produce visible bruising and can also cause lethal bleeding inside the body. Heavy blows may break bones. It is the pathologist's job to examine the body and figure out how the injuries were caused.

Internal Injuries

Heavy blows can damage vital organs. Many organs, such as the liver, contain large amounts of blood which escape inside the body and can cause death. When a pathologist examines the inside of a body, they look for internal bruising and bleeding.

Broken Bones

Battering someone with a blunt implement can break or crush a bone. The type of injury and the direction of the break can help the pathologist to decide how the break occurred. If the victim's head has been battered, his or her skull may be cracked or shattered, fatally damaging the brain.

The amount of damage inflicted by a blunt implement depends on the angle and force of the blow.

An X-ray of a broken leg shows the exact angle and site of the break.

Bruises

When something smashes against flesh, it breaks tiny blood vessels below the surface. The blood leaks out and causes a bruise. Pathologists look at the shape of the bruise to see if they can tell what made it. Was the victim stamped on, for example, or maybe hit by a car?

A punch in the face often results in a black eye.

BACK IN THE LAB

A pathologist examines bruises to see whether they formed before, during, or after the murder. Old bruises need to be identified and possibly excluded from the murder investigation. It is easy to identify a bruise made after the person has died, because the bruise will have bled less and be a light-brown color.

POISONS

Not all murders are instant. A poison is a substance that kills a person when it is ingested. Poisoning is a very old method of murdering a person and is much more rare than other forms of homicide. The most common way of administering a poison is to mix it into the victim's food or drink.

Common Poisons

Traditional poisons include arsenic and cyanide, but today, rat poison, morphine, and antifreeze are common, too. Arsenic has no taste and is hard to detect in food. It can kill within a few hours, days, or weeks, depending on the dose.

Detecting Poisons

A toxicologist is an expert in poisons who is called in when poisoning is suspected. Toxicologists look for traces of a poison in the body. They examine the contents of the stomach, the liver, blood, and urine. If the poison is no longer in the body, they look for damage to the body caused by the poison.

Poison could be secretly added to someone's drink by mixing it with sugar.

The berries, roots, and leaves of deadly nightshade, or *Atropa belladonna*, are all poisonous.

Likely Suspects?

A poisoner has to have access to his or her victim, so often family members are immediate suspects in cases of poisoning. Doctors and other medical staff have access to dangerous drugs. If several people die unexpectedly in the hospital, the hospital's staff may be suspected.

REAL-LIFE CASE

In 2006, Alexander Litvinenko, a former Russian spy, was poisoned in London. This was no ordinary poison, however, but a radioactive chemical called polonium-210, which was added to a cup of tea. Litvinenko became terribly ill, and because there is no antidote to the poison, he died 23 days later. A suspect was named, but he had already returned to Russia.

CHAPTER FOUR

FINDING THE MURDERER

The priority for police investigating a homicide is to identify and find the killer or killers. Deliberate, planned murders may have no witnesses. Gang killings, on the other hand, may have several, but the witnesses may be too scared to give evidence.

Getting Information

Police interview witnesses to find out what they saw. Did they, for example, get a clear look at the killer, or did they notice the color and make of a getaway car, or even the license plate number? If the killing happened in a public place, such as a store, gas station, or street, it may have been recorded on closed-circuit television (CCTV). Killers, however, are often aware of cameras and hide their faces.

Producing a Picture

The task of finding a killer is much easier if the police have a good image of them. Scientists use all the information available to produce a likeness. The likeness is circulated to police and may be published in newspapers or on television.

Before a suspect can be tried in a court of law, the police have to find and arrest him or her.

A witness to a murder in 2012 tells television reporters what she saw at the scene of the crime.

Asking the Public

Involving the public can produce vital evidence and links to a killer. People who did not witness the homicide may have other information that is useful in tracking down the murderer. Police sometimes appeal to the public through television shows. The television company reconstructs the crime and asks for any relevant information. The reconstruction may jog someone's memory and help to find a suspect.

CRACKED

Television shows invite viewers to phone in with information. Often, several people call in with information about the same person. The information may be anonymous, but it can provide just the lead the police need to crack the case.

IDENTITY PHOTOS

Getting a good, clear image of a suspect is critical for police. If the suspect has been convicted for previous crimes, the police will have a photograph on their database. There may also be a good image captured on a CCTV camera. If an image of a suspect does not already exist, one has to be created.

WANTED
FOR HOMICIDE / ARMED ROBBER

Suspect Description:
Sex: Male
Age: 31
Height: 5'10"
Weight: 180
Hair Color: Dark brown
Eye Color: Unknown

A wanted notice includes details of the crime and where it was committed, as well as an image, or likeness, of the suspect.

Making the Image

The technology for producing a likeness has improved enormously in the last 60 years. In the past, an artist drew a portrait of a wanted person, based on witnesses' accounts. In 1959, a Los Angeles policeman invented Identikit. This had a bank of ready-made drawings of different features, such as the mouth, eyes, and nose, from which the witness could choose. Today photographed features are adjusted on a computer to create an E-fit of a suspect.

Wanted for homicide and armed robbery of Kosak Convenience Store on ... ... and Higgins on the night of Sept. 24th. Suspect was last seen with a dark navy ... ... jeans, and black sweatshirt.
... have any information regarding this incident, call the Sheridan Falls Police

40 ... will remain anonymous.

The iris is the colored part of the eye around the pupil. Everyone's irises are different and cannot be changed.

Ageing an Image

In some cases a person may be wanted 20 or more years after the only available photographs were taken. Unsolved cases, called cold cases, are never forgotten. Using a computer, an expert can use a past photo to produce a new image of what the person is likely to look like several decades later.

Disguising Appearance

People on the run may go to great lengths to disguise their appearance. As well as changing the color and cut of their hair, some use plastic surgery to change their features. They may, for example, change the shape of their nose.

BACK IN THE LAB

Forensic scientists have worked with computer specialists to produce software that can identify the same person before and after plastic surgery. The program matches individual features, instead of attempting to match the whole face.

CAUGHT ON CAMERA

Killers and other criminals are more likely to be caught on camera than ever before. Surveillance cameras watch public places both inside and out. Smartphones take instant photos. These cameras can deter attacks, but they are also useful in identifying and tracking people and cars after the event.

Watching with Cameras

Surveillance cameras are video cameras linked to a central control room. The cameras may be watched by a guard or police officer, but they can also be monitored or scanned by a computer. This makes it much easier and faster to identify particular people or suspicious behavior. In recent years, the quality of the pictures recorded by surveillance cameras has become much clearer.

A surveillance camera on the side of a building records everyone who passes by.

Photographs taken on cell phones by passersby can provide investigators with important evidence.

License Plates

Traffic cameras monitor streets and roads. They photograph speeding vehicles and vehicles committing other traffic offenses. Traffic cameras can also be linked to a database of license plate numbers. This allows police to search for and track a getaway car or a car that was seen near the crime scene.

Cell phones

Cell phone cameras are very easy to use and take instant, good-quality photographs. Most people keep their phones on hand and can use them to record crimes and other events. Some people record crimes or criminals accidentally, when they are photographing something else.

REAL-LIFE CASE

On New Year's Eve in 2010, a man was shot while he took a photograph of his family outside their home in Manila in the Philippines. The gunman got away, but his image was later found on the camera. The final photograph clearly showed him, aiming his gun at the photographer, from behind the unsuspecting family.

WHAT NEXT?

Forensic scientists are developing more and better ways to catch killers. Computer software and databases store and monitor more information. Some people worry that the police can spy on us without our knowledge.

Tracking an Individual

Wherever you go and whatever you touch, you leave behind traces of your DNA. However, forensic scientists can now track people without having to find physical evidence. When you travel by car, the license plate is recorded on traffic cameras. Calls made on a cell phone can be easily traced, as can transactions made with a bank card. Wherever someone goes, a digital record is left behind.

Too Much Information?

As detecting and analyzing DNA becomes more reliable, a central database of everyone's DNA could be set up. Forensic scientists could then instantly identify anyone whose DNA was found at a crime scene. Most people agree, however, that such a database would invade a person's right to privacy.

When credit cards are used online, the computer records the details and the date and time it was used.

44

An electronic passport has a computer chip with a digital photo, so that a computer can quickly check the true identity of the passport holder.

Cell phone records show exactly where someone is at the time they make each call from the phone. These records are often used to support or destroy a suspect's alibi. An alibi is the claim that a suspect could not have committed the crime because he or she was somewhere else at the time.

Recording Guns

In the United States, the details of guns used in crimes are stored on a nationwide database. Since any gun can be identified from its unique rifling marks (see page 30), it would be possible for all guns to be registered before the gun was sold. Gun ownership laws are under review in the United States, with proposals to limit ownership of certain gun types following the 2012 Sandy Hook tragedy in which 20 children and six adults were shot dead.

GLOSSARY

artery a tube that takes blood from the heart to a particular part of the body

autopsy a medical investigation into the cause of death

barrel the part of a gun down which the bullet travels after it is fired

cartridge a container that holds a bullet and powder that explodes to fire the bullet

cell the smallest part of a living thing

circumstantial evidence evidence that shows a person could have been involved in a crime but does not prove it

closed-circuit television (CCTV) a camera or cameras linked to a television screen or computer screen

contaminated polluted

convicted found guilty of a crime

database information stored on a computer in such a way that it is easy to search and access

death penalty execution approved by the state

dental records records kept by a dentist that detail everything about a person's teeth

digital in a form that can be read or stored by a computer

DNA short for deoxyribonucleic acid, the unique code inside every human body cell that controls every element of how we look, such as the color of our eyes and hair

evidence information, objects, or substances that are related to a crime

fingerprints prints left by the tips of the fingers

gunshot residue the powder left behind when a bullet is fired from a gun

license plate a plate issued when a new vehicle is registered. The plate displays a number that is unique to that vehicle.

offenses unlawful acts

pathologist a doctor who examines a body to determine the cause of death

plastic surgery surgery that changes a person's appearance

radioactive giving off a type of energy that is particularly damaging to living things

reconstruct to rebuild a chain of events

rifling marks the scratch marks made on a bullet as it passes down the barrel of a gun

self-defense action taken to defend yourself from an attack

serial number a unique number given to an object

shell case the outside case of a cartridge, which remains after the bullet has been fired

software computer programs that tell a computer what to do

suicide when a person kills himself or herself

surveillance cameras CCTVs used to protect people and property

suspect a person whom police think may have committed a crime

treads the grooves cut into tires or the soles of shoes

vital organ part of the body, such as the heart, brain, or lungs, without which a person cannot live

FOR MORE INFORMATION

BOOKS

Cooper, Christopher. *Forensic Science.* New York, NY: Dorling Kindersley, 2008.

Romano Young, Karen. *Crime Scene Science.* Washington, DC: National Geographic Children's Books, 2009.

Royston, Angela. *Science vs. Crime.* New York, NY: Gareth Stevens, 2013.

Schulz, Karen K. *CSI Expert! Forensic Science for Kids.* Waco, TA: Prufrock Press, 2008.

WEBSITES

Get a very clear account of what forensic science is all about at:
idahoptv.org/dialogue4kids/season12/csi/facts.cfm

Find out all about the FBI at their interactive website for kids at:
www.fbi.gov/fun-games/kids

Play interactive games that allow you to choose various possibilities to solve the crime at:
www.museevirtuel-virtualmuseum.ca/sgc-cms/ expositions-exhibitions/detective-investigator/

INDEX